MW01517463

LOVE +

lifestyle

Inspiration for Women

Sept 9 - 15.

To Nikki:

It was amazing to Meet you. Wishing you endless Possibilities. Thank you.

LOVE +
lifestyle
Inspiration for Women

Ahava Chai Presents:
12 WOMEN + 12 STORIES *Love. Passion. Purpose.*

JANÉT AIZENSTROS

*Dedicated to the late Maya Angelou
the caged bird who now sings of freedom*

No part of this publication may be produced, stored in a retrieval system, or transmitted in any form or by any means, electronic, mechanical, photocopying, recording or otherwise, without written permission of the publisher.

For information regarding permission, contact Ahava Chai, LOVE+ Lifestyle Media Group. www.lovelifestylemedia.com

Publisher Prefix: 978-0-9920874
ISBN 978-1-77210-009-9

Copyright © December 2013 by Janét Aizenstros, All Rights Reserved.
Revised © September 2014 by Janét Aizenstros, All Rights Reserved.

Cover Design & Layout by Lauren Alicia

Published by Ahava Chai Publishing is a subsidiary of LOVE + Lifestyle Media Group and associated logos are trademarks and/or registered trademarks of Love + Lifestyle Media Group.

Love + Lifestyle Media Group is a registered company of Janét Aizenstros Omni Media Inc. All Rights Reserved.

"I CREATED THIS COMPILATION TO INSPIRE WOMEN WHO ARE ASPIRING TO CREATE WHAT THEY WANT TO EXPERIENCE IN BUSINESS, LOVE AND LIFESTYLE."

-JANÉT AIZENSTROS

TABLE OF *Contents*

Preface

THIS IS A NOTABLE COLLECTION of stories experienced and written by women who have excelled in their chosen field.

Professional and ambitious, these women have not only walked a path of their own choosing but have also masoned and laid down each stone.

Telling ones story is a powerful act. Revealing details from beginning to end takes courage simply because a story that ends in success rarely comes without a few chapters filled with strife.

Recounting a journey, the ups and the downs, brings about a vulnerability that exposes you. These women, undeterred, embrace their fragile moments. They've channeled it into strength to overcome the hardships they faced, allowing character to build and compassion to bloom.

Accomplishment is often laced with struggle; a very delicate state. In the course of a journey you are sometimes faced with circumstance, demons, judgment and fear. Negativity can be overwhelming, pulling you down into the depths of darkness. Staying close to the surface, keeping your head above it all, will seem impossible at times. You will search within for confidence and strength. Treading, maintaining and staying positive is taxing and you may find yourself on the edge of defeat despite your efforts but, that's when ambition finally kicks in.

Suddenly, you've taught yourself how to swim despite the crashing waves, the unknown and the circling sharks. You get to a point where you feel strong enough to reach your goals. When you see others struggle, barely staying afloat, you are compelled to share your strength. This is what this compilation is all about. These stories represent all women and are for all women. One of these stories can easily be told a hundred different ways by a hundred different women.

We are a collective that want to share our experiences, knowledge
and life lessons. These stories are meant to inspire. They have been
carefully chosen to inspire you, the reader.

Each one evolves and unfolds in its own time. They are all one in the same; beautifully human. Each of these women found their spark, their purpose. They decided to trust and believe in their ability to get them where they wanted to be. Faced with opposition and or discouragement they all managed to pull through.

The message is clear; do you want success? Yes? Now take a good look at yourself, make sure you are not the one holding yourself back.

Nobody is going to hand you success and it's not going to be easy but, turning your spark into a fire can be one of the most rewarding things you can do for yourself. You are not alone. These women have been exactly where you are, quell your doubts and get inspired!

-AYANNA DURANT, *Managing Editor*
LOVE+LIFESTYLE MEDIA GROUP

INSPIRATION FOR WOMEN

YASHEEKA*Sutton*

"In order to do anything in life, we have to put forth sincere effort. We have to train hard, then trust our training; formulate positive emotional energies around the task at hand then bang that ish out regardless of what it is. When we allow negativity to seep in, we doom ourselves to failure before we even get started. Don't do that to yourself. I draw my energy from the same G-dForce that you draw yours from. There's little difference between us. So use your energy well. Push yourself!! Fight through!! And because I do those things, I'll NEVER consider myself a loser or a failure. I'm a winner in the game of life because I don't quit!!!!! I may not hit the mark today with some things, but I'm a stay at it, if it's worth it, then eventually I'm a hit it, and hit it hard!!!!!"

-WILLIAM BLACKWELL [BWISEII]

I never once ran, I just kept walking with tears in my eyes, head held high and my chest slightly poked out. I walked straight into traffic– eyes opened and fully aware that I have just decided to give up. I never would have thought in a million years that I would end up in another country ready to surrender it all. I stepped onto the highway; the car that was supposed to hit me decreased their speed and slowed down, no horns, no screeching, and no yelling–as well as the cars that followed– they all just slowed down naturally. The driver who changed my fate gave me a look of disappointment as she mouthed "What Are You Doing?!"

Damn, what was I doing? Did I really just try to walk into traffic? I sprinted across the rest of the highway wiping back tears. Fuck! So you mean to tell me that I do have purpose and that I am needed here right now? Message received and not a moment too soon. Gee thanks.

Why was I in the middle of Montreal traffic trying to end it all? Let us rewind shall we? Senior year of undergraduate studies I was granted the wonderful opportunity to study abroad through an exchange program. I was delighted that I would be traveling not only out of the province but also, out the freaking country, flying for the first time ever in my life! It was no secret that my ambition has always been such an intrinsic additive to my existence as a child, teenager, student and now a young adult who's preparing to enter the real world. Therefore, once I was a confirmed exchanged student I leaped for joy because I was embarking on yet another journey and milestone in my life. I was an "accomplisher"–I accomplished and strived, and worked, and gained notifications, certificates, etc but deep inside I was not being fulfilled or satisfied by the labels and titles that I've earned over the years. Being that I was only a semester away from graduating with a bachelor's degree and a few weeks away from experiencing an entirely different way of life I began to question—what was my purpose again? I "knew" what labels and titles I wanted to earn but what really was my purpose.

It's amazing what you find out when you go within. The journey of Self Discovery could without a doubt be a scary journey when you think you are traveling alone, although, we are never truly alone. Could you imagine? Going [growing] through an enlightenment/awakening of higher consciousness and thinking you are the only one who is experiencing this shift–I too used to think I was the only one who was feeling this change that was happening to the mind, body, and spirit. You see, I had a major awakening that changed my life forever and it was faith (the size of a mustard seed) that moved mountains but on the other side of that faith was fear! That fear convinced my mind to tell my body to put one foot in front of the other, to move into traffic. What was I afraid of? I had everything mapped out and my life all pre-planned for the next 5-10 yrs in my mind. Did you catch that? In my mind – there was this ongoing strategic caveman way of thinking that in order to survive the world I had to "hunt, and kill, and cook, and win" in life. But where was the purpose? Where was the self-fulfillment – the compassion – the love? Where was the love of living life and loving what you live?

As merely visitors on this planet, I realized that we have been blessed with so much power that goes untapped due to a high level of ignorance. First thing first, I had to wipe away everything I thought I knew! I accepted the notion that I have been pulled into this illusion of The American Dream and it was completely up to me whether I was going to sink or swim. Well, I was never a great swimmer so I became a student - A student of life. This made me teachable and coachable. I have seen an increase in the amount of people now-a-days wanting to be the "expert" and wanting to show the world that they have arrived, that they have it "together" and this and that. [lol] Well, my notion was just the opposite of that; I didn't have it together and I had to stop convincing myself, and others, that I did. I just was not interested in trying to keep up with the Jones' because it seemed like it could be very a stressful and stress-filled façade to uphold. By design I'm a natural observer therefore learning by just watching came easy to me. Even as a child, I was told to "be seen and not heard", "speak when you are spoken to" and as a teenager I carried those themes with me well into my young adult life cycles.

Speaking of life cycles, I want to share some valuable knowledge with you that I learned early on about the lifespan of humans, which intensely lessened my stressful outlook on life by 100%. The first 28 years are experimental or what you would call "trial & error" where one is navigating through this plane LEARNING WHAT WORKS AND WHAT DOESN'T WORK FOR THEM–hence the trial and error stage. It's okay, you are supposed to grow through the first stage of your development making mistakes, and traveling down a whirlwind of experiments. The dilemma comes in when "society" tells you that by 24 you should have

(1) graduated from high school (2) graduated from a four year institution (3) landed a Corporate America job working at least 40 hrs a week (4) start planning to purchase a home and/or car (4) get married, (5) have children and last but not least–die, In that order! Sounds about right. Right?

Blah blah blah Talk about anxiety and the pressure to just simply live. You see this is the type of conditioning that would indeed have a 23 year old stressed and completely a mess because what I just mentioned above isn't necessarily a divine purpose. It's an outline; it's a paradigm. You see this is the conditioning from a society and an organized system. As I crossed the highway that day in Montreal, wiping back tears, therein–within my entire being was a shift. I began to shift from a place of uncertainty in which I could not display to family friends, classmates, etc. I could only continue to work with the changes of this shift. My transformation was an intentional one and now with a level of understanding that my journey was not only going to be different but purpose-filled. I had found purpose. Now life truly begins.

YASHEEKA SUTTON

RAMONA*Ostrander*
The Looking Glass

"Nothing is impossible, the word itself says 'I'm possible'!"

- AUDREY HEPBURN

We look at ourselves every single day. How often do you look for more than good hair, clean teeth, and signs of age or polished make-up? Imagine creating a looking glass that lets you see your life and inner-self beyond a superficial reflection. It is a priceless, one-of-kind, irreplaceable gift with an ever-escalating value – just like you. It helps bring your life purpose forward; defining your legacy to those around you. Each persons' looking glass is unique, but they all come with special instructions to help you shake the hold of your private burdens and redefine what you look for in your reflection.

To begin, there are four guiding words to creating and using your looking glass: honesty, clarity, authenticity and effort. Honesty is the best policy for health, heart & healing and drives the launch point of every journey into unleashing inner power. To demonstrate this process, I share with you my journey into the looking glass.

I am no different than any other woman in the world. I was born, exposed to a set of lessons and experiences and struggled with defining and delivering on my role as a daughter, wife, mother and woman; until my first days as a mother came to pass. These days were riddled with guilt and failure. Birthing had resulted in my child going to intensive care. I missed the opportunity to be the first to bond with her. Listening to my mother share the details of my daughter's reaction to their thunder-struck connection with each other twisted my insides with hurt, and an overwhelming sense that I had been upstaged by my Mom. It haunted me for months.

The pain grew and I toiled with the thought that I had lost my chance to ever be as good as my Mom, yet again. More educated, more experience, more in-tune with her instincts that are never wrong, meant my choices and decisions never rang the bell. My life was tied to living by my mother's opinions, never learning how to define myself.

Only this time, there was an impetuous murmur in my head, like a child trying to be heard over a boisterous room of adults, shouting at me to break this cycle of always falling short, always ignoring my own needs. I knew I could not lose this opportunity to define my own success. So, I wrote a letter to my daughter.

That letter proved to be the initial designing of my looking glass and began from a single source of self-honesty, my soul. I wrote, and I wrote and wrote and wrote. I rehashed every event in my life; trying to understand who I was, what I was made of and what I was made for, defining each failure on the road to that knowledge. My list was long and distinguished and hinged on the following benchmarks; what I had learned my Mom & Dad expected of me and my fear of what I would lose for not succeeding. In a universal twist of fate after 25 years of a less than ideal relationship with my father, he abandoned me. My relationship with my mother then veered into more and more dangerous territory of failure, fear of loss and yes, eventually a short period of abandonment. Plus, who doesn't have a closet full of relationship skeletons with men, women, friends, bosses, colleagues, self-esteem, confidence or self-worth?

So, what does a gal do with all that? As my baby slept quietly under my watchful eye, I realized I had two choices: walk down a bumpy path of little change and lose myself into an emotional abyss or look in the mirror at mySELF. OK. I picked-up the mirror! And for my next trick? Nothing. I had no idea where to move forward to after that choice was made. There had been honesty in that letter in a way I had never been honest with ME before. In reading the letter many times a new reflection of me surfaced from the years gone by; raising an awareness that delivered the next step. Drawing such profound personal clarity from this self-reflection helped to launch my journey; shooting me out of the gate at full speed and into a deep resentment and anger. This was not in the plan. I had envisioned a lovely meeting of the minds within my being encircled with Fairies, love dust and a whole bunch of sparkly items. What I endured was a sledgehammer, to the gut, as I released honest emotion and reality on my relationships with my parents. I never had a father outside the one I created within my own mind where I took his most inane gesture and turned it into PROOF that he loved me (this became the template I followed with a number of fellas I'll have you know). I was a nothing more than a blockade on the road detouring my mother's love away from him. Love was defined by my ability to maintain perfect obedience, endure mental and emotional challenges, threat of loss and succumbing to complete control over my life.

This secret recipe my parental unit crafted for earning and holding love in my life made me wrought with negative feelings for both of them. It also led me to defining my very purpose.

In this brilliant moment of personal clarity I vowed that I would never, ever leave a legacy of misguided love and detrimental cycles in my children's lives. I knew that my purpose was to be a role model of love and authentic intent. This would require me to disassemble myself from the way I had been raised to love; and rebuild myself layer by layer in front of my family with authenticity. It would require me to remain open on my shortcomings, successes, emotional needs and communication issues with those closest to me if I was to re-write the lessons of love of for my children.

Creating the legacy becomes simple when you know who you are looking at in the mirror. Stepping forward in life to evolve right in front of those you love only helps you embrace your full potential. Live your core values proudly, reflecting them in all you do and express. Live your personal clarity, be guided by honesty. Call a spade a spade when comes to your personal development and make choices to move you forward.

Several years have passed since I took a hands-on approach to developing my legacy. It has involved self-help, family communication and professional guidance. And, the work continues every day. My legacy revealed that it was not about hitting a level of notoriety or fame to make a difference, but simply living my life day to day. At the very foundation of this work it took a commitment to be authentic in all I do.

Living with authentic intent has become my new, and only, benchmark for personal success. Striving and reaching for authenticity takes daily, moment-by-moment effort. Like anything wonderful in life, it takes constant effort to bring success.

I am proud to have made the decision to take a long, caring look at my deeper reflection; and create a value within myself that can stand up to any challenge. Authentic intent has opened doors of opportunity in my relationships that I never thought imaginable. It has redefined my relationship with my mother and opened up an even deeper love between us that comes from a mutual respect for each other's reflections. It has enabled me to bring richness to my happiness, marriage, work and community. As I watch my babies sleep now, I can smile a genuine smile that we are working on a great legacy, together, as a family.

RAMONA OSTRANDER

TRUDY*Dixon*
Believe and YOU CAN!

"You can live your dreams if you want it bad enough."

- PERSONAL TRAINER

For as long as I could remember I never felt that I was a normal child. Let me explain that. I'm an identical twin. Yes I had the same sky-high dreams as other kids, I wanted to fly just like Superman. My sister wanted to be like Indiana Jones.

Our Mother involved us in sports from a young age, I think for several reasons, to keep us out of trouble and also to get us out of her hair for a few hours. So we competed in ballroom dancing, tried Judo for a few years, I also found a love for running. My first real life changer came while recouping from a back issue caused from a Judo session. I was lying on my back on the floor with my sister and Mother watching a movie called 'Lethal Weapon'. There is a great scene in it where the character of Riggs (played by Mel Gibson) manages to coerce a jumper of the roof in the most bizarre way. Seeing those two actors falling into a huge airbed looked like so much fun I turned to my Mum and blurted out 'I want to do that as a job!'

My Father was a Boat builder all his life, a true craftsman. My mother worked many jobs, most of them corporate. My older sisters had secretarial jobs. My Twin, who was by far more academic then I was, also wanted to work in the corporate world and here I wanted to jump off buildings and get dragged by horses.

About this time a major factor came into play that would shape my life forever. My twin unexpectedly died. At 13 other than grandparents, no one else that close to me had died. It was unexpected. I lost my partner in crime, my best friend and playmate. There was so much that

I was hoping we could do together, but sadly we never got around to it. I became the most talked about kid at school. It's times like these when you find your true friends. Till this day, they still protect me, stand by me and even now, remember the individual person that was my twin. A few years ago, out of the blue a Facebook page was built in her memory. That truly made me feel special to know that even for a short time, she made an impact on others lives. Could I be that lucky?

I was given freedom to just do my thing. But I didn't rebel, drink, smoke, or steal. I figured out how I could become that stunt person, or even a Phys Ed teacher. By now I was practicing more running, swimming, Martial Arts, Fencing, Gymnastics, Jousting, Trampoline, and by the time I could drive, I was learning to ride a motorbike. My Mother had been a biker riding a BSA, so could not object to me learning. My Father was the only one that could, but instead just asked that I be careful.

My career advisor at school suggested I find avenues into the stunt world. Surprising her with my career choice, did not impede her encouragement. I went on to study Performing Arts in college. I still have the form that she filled out during our meeting.

Not only did I find out what makes a great stunt person through reliable sources, I soon discovered after extensive research that a Performing Arts is not needed to become a Stunt Person, However, if I had not attended college, then the direction of my career may have gone a different way. The first life-changing opportunity that came along was from work experience. I managed to get the chance to work with two amazing women that owned their own theatre company. They specialised in stage combat shows. Two women physically beating the crap out of each other, but not actually hurting each other was a pretty impressive thing to see. They knew how to sword fight, just like in the swashbuckler movies I loved watching so much. I learnt so much from those ladies in regards to stunt fighting.

The second life-changing opportunity came up because of my tenacity to just keep plugging away until I got answers. I had written several letters to so many stunt professionals in the industry asking them for some small nuggets of advice on how to get into the business. What did I need to do to succeed? Was I on the right path?

I really didn't expect to get any replies. I know how busy those people can be. The last person I expected to hear from was the very man at the pinnacle of his career and considered the hardest working Stunt Person in the industry. Vic Armstrong, of Indiana Jones, James Bond, and Johnny Mnemonic, wrote me a personal letter stating that though he was extremely busy working on several movies, he would be back in the UK for a short time, and to give him a call.

Knowing his time was valuable I used it wisely. I had prepped. Questions were written down and I got my answers from the main man himself. No college needed but you did need several high level qualifications in specific sports. There it was, my new direction.

He did give me some words of warning though 'It's a tough industry to get into!" Most Stunt People come from a family of Stunt People. That's the way it's been for many years. So I was off again, scuba diving, continuing with all my other sports and working to pay for it all.

By now, I was actually teaching fitness. Having been an accounts clerk for 5 yrs, I left and started my own business. The only thing my Father asked was, "Can you make a living?" He really didn't understand that I was actually good at sports and teaching it too. The realization came one day in London. I had a tryout for the TV show 'Gladiators'. I travelled all the way back from my holiday in Turkey for 24 hours to go to this audition. My sister dragged my father along for support. My Mother was back in Turkey waiting for my return. My return flight cost more then the whole holiday, but my Mother, my top supporter all the way, was not about to let this opportunity go by, she foot the bill.

The audition was made up of an 800m run on a treadmill in under 3min, 5 chin-ups, horizontal ladder manoeuvre and climbing a 25m rope. Well I always loved gym class and I ran track in high school. The 800m was one of my signature events, so I knew I could do this. When my audition was over, I looked over to my sister and Dad. The look of pride on my fathers face made my day. There and then, he finally realized that I was an athlete and a fierce competitor. That memory stays with me even now. So when I call him from my new home In Canada, he still asks, "Are you making enough?" It's not necessarily a concern; he knows that I'm doing something I love as a way of life.

I never fully made it as a stunt person, Vic was right; it's a tough industry to get into. However, I was in a few movies, I helped other friends with their stunt work and I still got to meet some amazing stunt people over the years. I've done crazy stuff too, but I don't feel as if I failed. I've only ever wanted to tackle two careers; stunt person and physical educator. I became a personal trainer/ triathlon coach, so that I could still teach kids. I get to wake up each day and have fun at work and get paid to do it! I'm often inspired by my students and in helping my clients reach their health or fitness goals.

Even though my parents were worried about my career choices; and teachers and friends told me I couldn't do it; I always believed that I could. I got the last laugh in 2008, when I became the first female to attempt an event called the Enduroman - Arch to Arc a triathlon style event from London's Marble Arc to Paris' Arc de Triomphe. It is an 87mile run, 22mile swim, 180mile bike ride. Again, people thought I was mad, those that really knew me though, supported and helped me. I completed the run and bike sections, however the weather that year didn't co-operate for anyone to swim. The English Channel is a brutal body of water and conditions have to be just right or you are not allowed to even attempt the swim.

Most of my family goes along with what ever I say I'm going to do. I didn't fit the mould as a kid and I still don't. I've always followed the beat of my own drum. I have two wonderful nieces and friends with kids, and I hope I can inspire them to dream hard and work hard to accomplish what ever they set out to do. The only obstacles in life are the ones that you put there yourself. As a great friend once said to me, "You can live your dreams if you want it bad enough!"

TRUDY DIXON

TAMARA *Garrison-Thomas*
Wish it. Dream it. Do it.

"*I know the plans I have for you,*" announces the Lord.
"*I want you to enjoy success. I do not plan to harm you. I will give you hope for the years to come.*"

- JEREMIAH 29:11

In 2005, I sat on a couch in my Los Angeles apartment with a good teaching job, good pay, but feeling like I needed more. I couldn't pin point exactly what it was at that time but eventually I would figure it out. A few weeks after my epiphany, my father called and shared his new business venture idea with me and suggested that I partner with him. THAT WAS IT! I always felt the need to start a business, start something that I was responsible for building. What is interesting is that I always had a "side hustle" growing up. I was always selling candy, jewelry, composing music to sell, or offering music lessons. So I don't know what happened between my youthful ambition and this epiphany that made me forget about my true entrepreneurial spirit. After my dad called me, I partnered with him and we have been in business ever since. Entrepreneurship has always enticed me because of the control, flexibility, and freedom. I can work whenever I want, but know the amount of work I put in will lead to the results I get.

I understand that entrepreneurship is not for everyone. In the past eight years I have worked with many types of people and, unfortunately, not all people are capable of being entrepreneurs and that's ok. They just need to recognize it. However, there are some people that would be successful entrepreneurs that just haven't embraced it yet. Too many times I meet people who would be excellent business owners but they come up with too many excuses as to why they cannot be. Just remember, for every excuse there is an answer:

"I don't have the money to start." Well, that's what investors are for. "I don't know what kind of business I would have." There are coaches for that. "I don't think my spouse would approve." There are mediators for that and believe me once they see the fruits of your labor pouring in, they will approve then. "I don't know what my friends and family would think." They don't pay your bills. "What if I'm successful?" Then great! "What if I fail?" Then great!

The last two excuses are the most frequent ones I hear.

What if I'm successful? Honestly it boggles my mind that someone would be scared of being successful. Unfortunately, it happens and it can be our past that feeds our current fear. Our fear can also stem from the potential response from people we know. Isn't it interesting how people can put pre-determined limits on what they believe we are capable of doing? Isn't it amazing how we let what other people think affect our actions? I'm reminded of a quote by Deepak Chopra:

"What other people think of you is none of your business. If you start to make it your business, you'll be offended for the rest of your life." - Deepak Chopra.

We have got to stop letting what people say or do define our actions. It is a great accomplishment to become successful in business. And you should relish and cherish every memorable moment in the growth of your business.

What if I fail? Failure in something is inevitable. It's how you bounce back that brings success. Things won't always go the way you hoped they would. But the people that do not lose sight of their goals and dreams are the ones that will eventually have success. Keep the faith, find a good mentor, and try again.

Get rid of these excuses and embrace the entrepreneur within you. Avoid possible wasted time trying to do something other than what you know will change your life. Stop going through life, knowing it's not how you envisioned it and not doing anything about it. Are you living your life in complete denial, ignoring all the failures around you saying, "Oh well, that's life!" Or, are you stepping out on a limb, and taking actions to change your life? You should be taking action and doing things like:

+ Giving up habits you know aren't good for you.

 + Following through with personal goals

+ Doing all you can to get a financial promotion

 + Or even better, creating an exit strategy and taking steps to FIRE YOUR BOSS!

One of my favorite quotes is, "If you will do for a season what others won't, you can live the rest of your life like others can't. It's not a matter of whether you can or can't, it's a matter of whether you will or won't." ~Unknown

Find your entrepreneurial spirit and mold yourself into a success story.

SHARON*Smith Stewart*

"A journey of a thousand miles begins with a single step."

- L A O - T Z U

The day that I decided it was time to move my life forward and let go of all the demons in it was the day I allowed myself to become the true me. The feeling that I got provided me with a calmness that only happens once you allow it to break beyond the pain, and shackles that have held you back up until that moment. This freedom released the harmony and oneness my heart and soul were waiting to receive and the greatness that was meant for me.

I had spent my entire 40 years doing the right things, living the straight and narrow. I went to church every Sunday, applied myself in school and was a really good person to everyone around me. With all that I did through the years, my reward was heartache, abuse and loneliness.

Looking back, I realized that I used all of my accomplishments to hide behind the one thing that held me back from taking the real risks I wanted to take to make me shine. You see, I was a very scared child, who became a frightened teenager and then a terrified adult. The big dark secret, the one thing that held me back was SHAME. The shame of a hard childhood, the shame of what happened behind closed doors and the fear that someone would find out. It was as though I was pregnant, pregnant with fear.

As history would have it, as for many other families, my parents were very hard working people who immigrated to Canada to make better lives for their children. With this transition, came the stress, which in my families case, translated into violence and an ongoing cycle that lead to a vicious childhood programming of fear and shame.

I remember the walk home and how it made my heart beat and my palms sweat. Each step made my feet feel heavy and the worry of what was behind the door was so intimidating. In my house, the fights were huge and the bruises were even bigger. Everyone on the street heard the arguing, crying and saw the fear. Yet every day we got up and smiled as though everything was perfect. I smiled when my heart ached, and laughed when I wanted to cry.

My whole life felt this way, the need to want to cry. I'm not sure if it was the fact that everyone in my family modeled the same fear and shame. The men were all adulterers and the women were caught in the midst of the same horror. Not sure if it was the loss of my best friend to cancer at 13 or the separation of my friends due to the men in my family behaving inappropriately or the permanent black eyes that I saw my mother cover up every day with makeup to hide her shame. Not sure, but I always wanted to cry.

I really can't remember the first time I heard her cry, but they were always gentle sobs. His arguing was loud, vulgar and powerful and the crashing of objects and fists were deafening, yet the sobs remained soft so not to worry us with anything that was happening outside our bedrooms.

When I reminisce of those days, I still can feel the sensation of my heart beating with such despair that I thought it was going to jump out of my body as I made my way down the steps as an eight year old child to help my mother clean up yet another mess. I remember staring up at her pretty face that was swollen and bloodied as we quietly put things back in their place as if it were a Saturday cleaning day.

She would send me to my room and I would lie near the door, or put my ear to the vent that was directly above their room or just hide under my bed that night because the night before, I hid and fell asleep in the closet and did not hear her cry. It was this and many other secrets that made me lonely.

Despite all of the darkness that constantly engulfed me, a solitude or bright cloud did exist for me during this part of my journey. It's comfort came through being around my older brother. His world was always peaceful and serene. He never realized the intrinsic beauty of this silence, as it unfortunately was his reality.

My brother's deafness created the arena for me to dream and design without interference or contamination creating a world of calm. It allowed for me to hear God's natural grace and appreciate what was around me.

His Lack of hearing prevented him from being tarnished and frightened by the very world in which he existed within our home. His inability fed my imagination and my disconnected spirit allowing me to construct and connect our two worlds in a way that kept him safe. I yearned for the family that laughed at silly jokes and talked, rather than yelled. Or like the characters in *The Cosby Show* who shared stories of positive experiences and instilled strength and confidence in their children. I was able to tell him stories of grandeur through sign language that would light up his eyes and think he lived in a perfect world. This helped to heal my soul and saved him from the sounds that so often deafened me. I loved existing in that time and needed it as a mechanism to prepare for what was going to happen next.

Although, I believed it to be a blessing in disguise, that part of my journey was difficult and transitioned me into someone who withheld or overindulged emotions, made it impossible to have healthy attachments to people and prevented opportunities to build trusting relationships. I found myself clinging to those that showed me attention, not the way that one would think. Nothing that sent me on a path to do wrong or to behave immorally, but, to individuals that made me feel the freedom I so longed for. I began to sing and would eventually get a record contract to which I would decline. I would have the opportunity to travel but would shy away from it. I would be given the opportunity to have true love only to destroy it with insecurities. These insecurities kept me in a turbulent marriage that was bridled with affairs and brought me back to the childhood spot of feeling shamed, lonely and abused.

Coming full circle, I now saw that it was time to birth and release that child that had developed, grown and protruded in front of me all these years. I desperately needed to cut the cord that has for so long been a dysfunctional lifeline that kept me closed in its grips.

With each push, revelations began to appear. I had realized that I cannot control what others have done or carry the blame for not being able to prevent what had happened. These events were a part of a bigger plan in which I was asked to play a role. I began recognizing that the shadows of fear need not be debilitating but a source that strengthens me to conquer the things that I once dreaded. I pushed out the anger, I screamed in pain the release of hate and in the end I birthed something new. The beginning of a true me.

This birth has been a ray of sunshine that now brightens my every step. I've used those challenges as mantras or tattoos that show that all struggles are for the best as they build character and reveal strength that you may have never known you had. I am now the CEO of my own youth organization which helps to transition adolescents into healthy adults, I have established an incredible new relationship and appreciation with my mother who herself has morphed into a precious stone of beauty and durability. I have released the power that many had over me by forgiving the people who hurt me over the years.

These steps have helped me to effectively transfer without bias the knowledge that has come from those childhood wounds to my two beautiful children. My daughter is able to see how to reprogram her thinking and create the world in which she wants to live. She is able to realize that self-love beats the love of anyone and without it you will allow someone to interpret who and what you should be. My son witnesses the strength of women and his role in loving and protecting them. He is also learning the importance of trust and forgiveness and that love is beautiful.

For me, this new chapter of my life now has me excited for what the future holds. I welcome challenges and no longer fear defeat as I see that this journey as one in which I can build an army and we can conquer the world. Although my journey is just beginning, each step is bringing me closer to the divine being the universe intended me to be.

MOIRA*Sutton*

Awakening Your Passions and Life's Purpose

"Let your passion lead you to your purpose."

- OPRAH WINFREY

Passion is the greatest energizer for us to live life fully and create success in our lives. Passion is energy and there is a high frequency around the feelings you experience when you are in this space. Passion begins within you and connects you to your true, authentic, spiritual self and you get excited. How do you know you are passionate about something? You can recognize passions by noticing things about yourself, such as you might start talking more quickly, have more animation in your movements and gestures. Can you remember a time when people said your face just "lit up!"? Well, that's it. When you get excited and can't stop thinking about something you are going to be doing or someone you are going to meet then that's passion! You wake up in the morning and you think about what a great day you are going to have, whether you are working or going on vacation. That's living a life of passion.

Life constantly sends us signals of what we are passionate about, what people, situations and things 'light us up'. We find ways to spend more time in those thoughts and doing those activities. I have spent my life helping people reconnect to their passions and discovering their unique purpose in their lives. Passion is what gives us joy. The people around us feel this passionate shift in us and want to experience it; be part of it. The people that want to share my passion are also the most fun for me to be around. Since they are attracted to me and I am attracted to them the cycle continues.

When I am in those moments of passion I follow them. I have made a career out of them. As a young woman it started with wanting them. As a young woman it started with wanting my degree in psychology; I knew this was the perfect choice for me and that I always wanted to work with people to help them overcome their problems, to discover what brought them joy and to discover tools to help people generate their own joy everyday. I could help them move beyond obstacles, challenges, fears and negative beliefs. I wanted to help them step into a bigger version and vision in their life – one of happiness, joy, love and fulfillment.

I followed my intuition and it led me on a winding wonderful learning journey. When I was in my 20's I met my now lifelong friend Judy Sherman, who is an artist, teacher and an entrepreneur. Through her stories and her quest for professional freedom, I had one of those 'aha' moments Oprah talks about. I saw the possibility for me to become an entrepreneur and use this as a vehicle to share my passions, purpose and vision with the world.

One of my greatest passions is traveling around the world, visiting new places, learning about their cultures and meeting their people. I felt that if I was an entrepreneur, I would have the freedom to travel, to create, to work with whom ever I choose and be on my own time schedule. Life was about to transform me and I was about to step into a whole new way of being in the world.

My first entrepreneur business was based in computers and administration. Judy (yes my best friend) was also a designer and she has designed many of my cards throughout the years. For my first business card, I wanted something that reflected my integrity, passion and skills, my strongest professional assets, to every client. Both Judy and I were incredibly excited to get started. We decided that everything I did in my personal and professional life should be projected effortlessly through my branding so, we came up with the company name "Personal Best."

In those days we did not have the Internet. I would drive around town for hours and write down names of companies just to find clients. I also used the phone book. Yes it may seem ancient now with all the iPads, smartphones and new technology available. I would then create a proposal. I mailed these to hundreds of companies offering my services. It was a lesson I almost forgot years later. When I was getting started I spent almost all my time contacting potential clients or sharing what value I could bring – with just about anybody. I intuitively knew it was, and still is, the heart of any business. Whenever I let those efforts slip as the years went by, my business slowed.

My first client was an Accounting Firm in Toronto at Yonge and St. Clair. I remember working all night on the project to meet the deadline and then drove to the location in the early morning to drop off the work. There was a great bakery at this location and I bought yummy cakes to take home and to celebrate my first cheque written to my first company "Personal Best". I can still taste that chocolate cake and it still makes me smile. From that time on I have never looked back at making the decision to start my own company be the founder and CEO of my business and my life!

I have had the honour to create great value for people and bring them joy. I could take time off to travel, meet with friends, and hang out with family on flexible times. I got to follow all of my passions. It's been pure bliss.

My business was a success and it continued to grow. Then along came an innovative and exciting new field, Neuro Linguistic Programming or NLP. It was like magic. I was so fascinated that this approach to communication, psychotherapy and personal development helped me make better choices. The more I studied and began coaching with NLP the less time I seemed to have for my computer business. Before long it became clear I was at a fork in the road.

We all have choices on our life's journey and passion often dictates them. That was the case for me. My new passion for NLP and helping people with this new skill started to take over. This meant new contacts, new clients, new friends and new adventures. One of my clients was extremely unhappy in her relationship with her boyfriend She did not have healthy boundaries and allowed him to direct her life. She had low self-esteem and very poor confidence. She did not know how to change this situation. She wanted a new and better direction to take in her life. Through our work together, she began to see the light at the end of the tunnel. She took back her power and decided that she wanted more for herself including a relationship of mutual respect, love and passion. She had her breakthrough and moved on to another relationship, one of joy, love and passion.

In a way this was predictive of deeper things to come. One of the fundamental presuppositions in NLP is "The Map is not the Territory." We experience the world in our own unique way and see what we are conditioned to and want to see. The reality is often quite different, especially when things get tough. Sometimes we need help to see a bigger, more honest and usually more beautiful picture. I provided that help and loved doing it.

Later in my career I began to really understand how important it is to make time for my clients to blast through their limiting beliefs, attitudes, habits and much deeper blocks. This enabled them to breakthrough to living their life with passion and loving who they are.

As you know, one of my BIG Passions is traveling. I had just received my Australian visa. I was ready to go to Australia, half way around the world! Then the opportunity to train in NLP in Toronto presented itself. What to do? I really wanted to do the NLP training in the Fall and I even explored taking the training in Australia, however I really liked the teacher in Toronto. I decided I would change my plans for now, go to Europe for the summer and come back in the fall to take the course and become a Certified NLP Practitioner.

This was one of those turning points in my life. I followed my passion. When I made the decision and took action to follow through, another door opened! Not only did the one year NLP Certification course open up a new world for me, I met the love of my life – my husband Cliff. A few months into our dating, Cliff asked me to meet him in London, Ontario and he had a surprise (I love surprises) so I drove out later that day. He shared an exciting idea that was soon to become a reality.

Together we explored the idea of living on a sailboat in the Caribbean islands. We decided we would sell most of our furniture and create a plan together to fly to Florida and purchase our sailboat. We did not know when we were going to come back and loved the 'not knowingness' adventure and freedom! Cliff quit his job and we were now both officially on the path of Entrepreneurship.

We found our boat 'Felicity' in Clearwater, Florida. We stocked her up and off we went. We were on our new adventure that would last for just under one year. Pictures of funky fun people we met, wonderful lobster dinners, snorkeling and beautiful beaches are still fresh in my memories daily – over twenty years later.

Cliff and I now speak on cruise ships every year as Enrichment Speakers and we continue to visit the islands that we love and we are passionate about sailing, and the adventure. We have even both sailed on America's Cup racers in beautiful St. Martin!

Back home in Canada I began a journey of years of training in various alternative health programs. One of my passions is teaching and with most of the courses I was certified in, I would continue on to the teacher's level. I wanted to bring more to my clients and offer them choices and combinations of my training. I am a Usui Reiki Master; Karuna Reiki Master, Certified Reflexologist, New Decision Therapy, Behavioral Certified Kinesiologist, Aromatherapist, New Decision Therapist, Conscious Core Transformation Teacher and a Remote Viewer. I have Certificates in Robbins Madanes Strategic Intervention Coaching, Ontario Group Fitness Leadership Training and Marriage Education & Divorce Prevention. I love that I can offer my clients a variety of modalities to help them create the life they truly want, a life with passion and purpose.

So, how do you discover your passions and life's purpose? It is important to discover what comes naturally to you. I connect with people and one of my passions is researching and interviewing people who share their life stories. I discover what inspires them, what challenges have they overcome in their lives and what makes them happy. Through these stories I learn how they empower themselves and the people they love to move through the problems they face in their lives.

As we share experiences and I share the experiences of others, they discover that if you reframe challenges, obstacles and your biggest problems into life's gifts, you can learn from this, grow and become more in your life. This is what transformation looks like. Think of a beautiful butterfly who started as a caterpillar then transformed. The butterfly cannot go back to being a caterpillar.

One thing I know, when you decide you want to change something in your life things start to happen. Perhaps you want a loving relationship, to lose weight, to have more clients, to change careers, to move to a new home, to start writing or to travel more. Whatever it is you want the first step is to make the decision. Immediately there is a shift in your energy and the right people, circumstances and events begin to show up in your life. Your world comes into alignment with you, a newly transformed butterfly.

KEITIAUNNA*Howard*

"Success is not measured by how much you have, but by what you've done with the gifts that you've been given."

\- KEITIAUNNA HOWARD

I saw a post on FaceBook that said" If we're made in God's image, then why can't I put lotion on my own back?" Someone responded to that persons post and said that it was God's way of reminding you that you can't do everything alone.

I agree 100% with the fact that you can't do everything alone in life, however this pushed me to dig a little deeper. Several years ago, I was in a relationship and ironically, the guy would lotion my back for me each morning. It just became our thing, even though I'd leave for work before he would, each morning, he'd wake up to lotion my back. Now that we're no longer in that relationship, I've learned how to lotion my own back – and although it may not be done as well as if someone was doing it for me, I do a very good job of it.

So what's the lesson here? In life, we learn how to do things that would usually be done by our mate or may be done better if our mate did it for us. That doesn't mean that we no longer need the mate to do those things; we've just taught/conditioned ourselves to improvise in the mean time. We still need to be sure to keep in mind that just because we can do something ourselves, doesn't mean that it wouldn't be better if someone was there to do it for us or with us. So the next time, you reach your arms around and struggle to put lotion on the middle of your own back, remember, although you can do things in life on your own, it's so much better when we all work together.

You may be wondering why I shared that story. Marianne Williamson said, "You must learn a new way to think before you can master a new way to be." See how a simple post about lotion caused me to dig deeper and find a greater meaning? I was able to see myself in that situation. I've been through a lot. I had learned how to lotion my own back but that post reminded me that I couldn't continue blocking people out. Instead I needed to change my way of thinking and embrace my life as it had been.

I grew up in a single parent household, graduated high school with honors and went off to college. My sophomore year, I got pregnant with my son. December 15, 2000 I gave birth to a beautiful little boy. As excited as I was, I also found myself depressed. I was the first out of my circle of friends to have a child. I was confused and scared. I feared that I would have to drop out of school, but thankfully I had a Dean of Students that taught me not to let my current situation dictate my future. June 2003, I walked across the stage and graduated with a BA in Broadcast Communications, it only took me one extra year than I had originally planned when I started college. In 2008, I completed a Masters Degree program earning a M.S. in Marketing & Communications. My son was healthy and happy and life was going well. When I was 30, I met a guy and thought we were in love. Shortly thereafter, I found out I was pregnant; this time I was having a little girl. While I was pregnant with my daughter, I quickly learned that I was not in the best environment for my son, my unborn daughter or me and I made the decision to end the relationship. I found myself 30 years old and a single mother of not one but two children. I'm not going to lie, it's been a very hard journey, but I refused to quit. January 2012, I started my own non-profit organization called Successful Single Moms, LLC.

I don't list my degrees and accomplishments to toot my own horn; I do it to show that you can't let anything stop you from achieving your dreams in life. Never would I have imagined when I sat there facing my biggest fear of telling my mom I was pregnant at age 20, that thirteen years later I would have two degrees, two amazing children, completed two leadership academies, a non-profit organization and be writing a book! I didn't start Successful Single Moms because I knew everything about being a single mom. In fact, I am still learning each and every day what it takes to be a mom. I started it because I know the experiences that I've gone through, and I know that I couldn't have made it without having people in my corner. I realized that not all women have people in their lives to support them and connect them with the right social agencies or people who will give them opportunities. I realized that some women who have children feel they are all alone, and they just need someone who understands what they are going through. I realized that the number of single moms is growing by leaps and bounds every single year, but the number of organizations created to assist those moms is dwindling.

So how did I do it? To be honest, it was only by the grace of God that I stand where I am today. But as I sat down and thought about where I started, where I am now, and where I am going in the future, I realized that there are eight things that I've incorporated into my life and I'd like to share those with you.

1. Spend time with God or in meditation: Prayer is not only

only talking to God, but also more importantly, listening to what He has to say to you. It's an opportunity to get direction for your life. Meditation or quiet time is equally as important. The key is to keep positive thoughts flowing through your mind during the day.

2. Forgive yourself: Ladies, we are our own worst enemy…no one is holding us responsible for the mistakes of our past except us. To be honest with you, this is the hardest one for me. Once we get to the point where we can move past the mistakes that we've made, we can embrace our future and takes steps to a better life for not only our children, but most importantly, a better life for ourselves.

3. Believe in yourself – If you don't believe you can do it, who else will?

4. Surround yourself with people you trust who believe in you – When you doubt yourself, you have to have someone in your corner that you can be honest with. That you can say, I'm scared or I don't know if I can do this or I need help. These are people that will allow you to have that quick moment of fear and then remind you to put your big girl panties on and do what you're supposed to do.

Dan Brown said, "Men will go to far greater lengths to avoid what they fear than to obtain what they desire." Don't allow your fears to paralyze you and keep you from moving forward. Fear is normal, but push past it.

5. Find or get reacquainted with your dream - What is your passion? What is the one thing you would do every day for free if you could (but you'd actually love to be getting paid for it)?

1. What do you need to achieve your dream? Do you need to go back to school or take a few classes? Do you need to look into relocating? How much money do you need for your dream? Are there organizations in your city that can help you? If your dream is to start a business, do you have a business plan? Do you even know what a business plan is or looks like? You have to research your craft.

2. Study your dream - who else is doing it, how is yours different. Is there someone you can shadow or can you get a mentor

3. Set aside time for your dream - During the day, I work my emails, I post information to help our moms, I forward job postings and I'm also available for phone calls for moms in need. In addition to that, I usually spend from 9:30-11:30pm during the week working on Successful Single Moms. On Friday nights I may spend longer. Unless we have a workshop or event, I try to take off Saturday and Sundays, but even on those days, I may jot down some notes using the notes app or voice record on my phone.

6. Create a vision board - The idea behind a vision board is that when you surround yourself with what you want to be, what you want to have, what you want to change in your life and how you want to live, your life will begin to change to match those desires. The vision board gives you a visual representation and reminder of your goals, dreams and aspirations and by looking at these things every day, you bring them to life and make them your reality.

7. Trust yourself/trust your instincts – you can call it your gut, your women's intuition, your conscience, or any other name. No matter what you call it, learn to tune in to it and learn to trust it. When we're about to make a decision, we quickly weigh it in our minds before we act. If it feels wrong, then it's probably going to be wrong. Learning how to pay attention to the small voice on the inside of you can keep you from making a lot of mistakes. Oprah Winfrey said, "Learn to let your intuition—gut instinct—tell you when the food, the relationship, the job isn't good for you (and conversely, when what you're doing is just right)."

8. Have fun, enjoy life! - Relax – Make time for yourself! Get a massage or hang out with your friends. If you can't afford something major, do something smaller...go to the massage school or the nail school. Or maybe plan a small get together with your girlfriends and have everyone bring a dish. For me, I LOVE spending time with my girlfriends! I'd love to do something huge, but to be honest, when we all decide to get together and everyone brings something to eat, we sit and laugh and swap stories and have a good time. Spend time making memories with your children. Create a happy and peaceful environment at home. We only get one life, if we spend too much of our life working or fussing with our children or wallowing in self-pity, we'll miss out on all that life has to offer us.

Asha Tyson said, "Your Journey has molded you for the greater good, and it was exactly what it needed to be." Don't think it's too late. Don't think that you've made too many mistakes. It took each and every situation you have encountered to bring you to the now. And NOW is

RIGHT ON TIME. Don't allow yourself or anyone else to convince you that just because you got a little bit off track, that doesn't means all hope is lost. Life will get rough sometimes and there's absolutely nothing that we can do about that. Just remember that the ups and downs of life are all a part of your journey. Life is what you make out of it. Allow your past to push you into your destiny. There are dreams locked up on the inside of each and every one of you and there are people in this world waiting for you to put some feet to those dreams. Don't allow fear to paralyze you from moving forward. Push fear out of the way and begin to push forward.

You can do it!

You can succeed!

You are a woman of Greatness!

KEITIAUNNA HOWARD

CAROLYN*Dickinson*
Passion & Purpose

"They may forget what you said, but they will never forget how you made them feel."

- CARL W. BUECHNER

Is passion bestowed on us or can we learn to be passionate about something?

Passion is "a term applied to a very strong feeling about a person or thing. It is an intense emotion, compelling feeling, enthusiasm or desire for something." (Dictionary)

Passion can be that energy that can fuel your project, ignite and motivate you; it has a similar role to inspiration. When you have the opportunity to engage in something you are passionate about, it's like a force of nature that is influenced by things that extend outside your self. It feels like everything else around you fades into the background, time recedes and everything flows. Passion is something that most people should strive to have.

Following your passion is like taking a leap off a cliff, pulling the cord to your parachute and gliding through the air while the wind pushes you through the sky – flying.

Purpose is "the object toward which one strives or for which something exists; an aim or a goal." (Dictionary). Purpose is that feeling of knowing, in your heart, that you are doing what you are meant to do. To some this may sound corny, but the moment one realizes their purpose the feeling is amazing. Everything just flows. Doors open up, people offer their support and people help you follow your purpose.

Often, passion is purpose and purpose becomes our passion. If this happens, then you are in a wonderful place. Don't get caught up with what you think you should do or even what others think you should do. When you are truly passionate about something you can't wait for someone to ask you what you've been doing, and when they ask you can't help but smile – your eyes light up and your heart races for the opportunity to share what you do. Your excitement is so contagious that anyone listening to you wants to know how to help you or be a part of what you are doing. You get up in the morning and you can't help but smile because it is a new day to do what you love!

I have been very fortunate over the last 5 years to meet some amazingly successful entrepreneurs. One of the things these people all have in common is that they all started their business by discovering a neglected niche in the market, something that was missing in their lives. These entrepreneurs used the skills they were great at and made their businesses come to life and prosper. Some found their purpose and by caring for that purpose, building it and prospering in it, that business became a passion. For others, they knew what their passion was and their passion lead them to discover their purpose. Whatever the way, these people are blessed and you can be too.

While growing up, my parents had the philosophy that both girls and boys should have the same skills, whether that was doing the laundry or changing the tire on the car. Because of them, I become very good at putting things together and fixing things. But a few years back, I participated in an exercise called the Kolbe ATM Index. Kolbe WisdomTM determines your conation; your willful determination to act on instinct. When I received my results from the Kolbe ATM Index, I was surprised to find that although I was very good at putting things together,

I really did not like doing it. The question asked of me was this, while you are putting a piece of furniture together what is going through your mind, does it sound something like, "when will this be over?" I was shocked because that is exactly what I would be thinking! When is this going to be over or what can I do to make this go faster so I can do something else. I really don't like working with my hands.

We all have moments when we wonder what we are doing and why we are doing it. When I go out to a networking events and someone asks me what I do, at that very moment I can feel myself shift, the excitement rise inside me and an amazing energy emanate from my body. At that moment I am reminded why I do what I do and why I love what I do.

The thing that saddens me the most is that there are many people that will never experience feeling their passion or living in their purpose because they keep finding reasons why they can't – standing in their own way.

What are you willing to do to live your passion?

Passion has the ability to change and shift as you grow and change through life. People are sometimes too busy looking for things to be presented in a pretty little box all ready to go. Well my friends, it's not always like that.

My passion started out with the desire and love to help others – especially children. It came from the fact that I love their honesty, simple view on life and the world around them. It is amazing to sit back and really listen to a child talk or share an experience they had and their view on how it all happened – without judgement. At a very young age I loved babies and hanging out with little kids. I started with babysitting when I was 14 years old, then in my early 20s I volunteered for Children's Aid followed by inspiring students with learning disabilities. It was an amazing opportunity to guide them in finding their power and the support they needed to be their best.

In my early 20's I decided to study Early Childhood Education and from there, a degree in psychology. School was very difficult for me having a learning disability, but I knew what I wanted and because I was passionate about the direction I was taking. I found ways to make it work and people to help me achieve my goals along the way. The amazing thing people do not realize about learning disabilities is that there is no lack of intelligence; we just see things and process information differently. The key is to find the right path for each person and the brilliance will rise to the surface, much like finding your passion. I spoke to students and parents of children with learning challenges and I loved the look on the faces of the audience when I was done. I would have line ups of people waiting to speak to me and thank me for sharing my story, giving them hope and showing them that truly anything is possible.

One of the most exciting things for me is that I have been blessed with two amazing little girls and that I will have the honour of supporting them in exploring and finding their passion and purpose. What a gift!

I live my life with the purpose of supporting and coaching moms and women in transition from corporate to entrepreneurship – from stay at home mom to stay at home mom entrepreneur, from maternity leave trying to find a way to stay home and those entrepreneurs looking at becoming a mom. I still have a passion for children, but I would like to incorporate other aspects of what I do into that passion, as children are our future. If you look closely, the common denominator for me is the ability to help others reach their goals and find their passion and purpose in whatever way I can. Now, that excites me! Touching the lives of others, and supporting them in reaching their passion and purpose is a gift and I feel honored to have been given this amazing opportunity in my lifetime.

Don't let life pass you by and ignore what makes you happy. You have a purpose and a passion. Its time to find out what that is. And better yet, how can you support someone in finding his or her purpose and passion? When we touch someone's life in a positive way we teach them to do the same, and so on. What an awesome way to make the world a better place one step, one story, one person at a time.

How will you choose to live and honor your life?

"When work, commitment, and pleasure all become one and you reach that deep well where passion lives, nothing is impossible."

-Nancy Coe

*Kolbe ATM Index and Kolbe WisdomTM are registered trademarks of Kolbe Corp.

CAROLYN DICKINSON

BRENDA*Foreman*
Be Careful What You Ask For

"Take the first step in faith. You don't have to see the whole staircase. Just take the first step."

- DR. MARTIN LUTHER KING, JR.

It was Fathers' Day and I spent the day with my Dad at his church and then we had brunch. When we got back to his house, he offered me a drink and I opted to take it with me to enjoy after my shower, while I read my book in my favorite chair.

Since my girls were with their dad, I could enjoy a few hours on my own, which I was looking forward to (or was I?). The months leading up to that day had been the longest, most gruelling months of my entire life. Everything that could go wrong went wrong. Every time I thought that things couldn't possibly get any worse...they did. I went from owning properties, investments, a nice car, money in the bank, having a beautiful loving happy family to being bankrupt, and in debt. I no longer had my family, I was now on my own with two little girls that needed me so much and I felt like giving up. Until this point I had not yet experienced such intense pain or emotions. Everything hurt, I couldn't cry anymore. I couldn't pray anymore. I found myself questioning if there was a God, no one heard my prayers, and no one was listening. I was alone. I wished for a broken limb, something that I could physically feel or see. I didn't want to feel anymore. I wanted to be numb. Everyday I woke up and painted a smile on my face so that my beautiful girls could see a strong woman who could overcome anything, while inside I wanted to die.

My father and I drove to my building in silence. The closer we got the more I dreaded going home to an empty apartment that was once full of life, love, laughter and a family that I could call my own. I was suddenly feeling a multitude of emotions; alone, abandoned, betrayed, hopeless...

There was a sudden downfall with heavy gusts of wind as we approached the building. I said goodbye to my father, ran into the building and unto a full elevator. My journey would end on the 23rd floor. I was in a daze as the elevator stopped, opened and closed numerous times on the way to the top. The doors closed for the last time. Only my next-door neighbor and myself were left on the elevator. It started to move. Number 22 lit up, there was a sudden jolt, the lights went out and then we stopped.

We were so close! What happened? We were not quite on floor 23. I could feel the elevator rocking on the cables with the strength of the wind, we were terrified. Instinctively we reached for each other in the dark. OMG, what should we do? I pulled my phone out for light. "Try the emergency button." she said. Nothing happened. Her phone had no reception, so I tried mine. Yes! I had reception...Call 911 she said. I did and it worked! "Help us, we are trapped in the elevator!" I said to the voice on the other end of the line. "Slow down ma'am, where are you? We'll send someone right over, please stay calm..." I tried my father's number as soon as I hung up the phone, he answered. As told him what happened, he turned around and waited downstairs while the fire department worked on the elevator.

What felt like hours at that time, turned out to be about 40 minutes. Forty minutes spent huddled on the floor with my then neighbor, now friend, praying, crying confiding in each other about our life experiences.

We were both dealing with so much at that exact moment, it was as if we needed each other and didn't even know it. I had no idea of the hardship and pain she was going through. So involved with my own survival, I was unaware of others. Although she could hear everything through the thin walls, she'd said nothing before now. She spoke to me like someone who really cared. She said, "I can feel your pain, I know your pain, I could hear so much of what you endured, through the walls. It's better that you are alone now. Focus on your children, focus on taking care of yourself, and start over, you can do it." I was shocked, but also relieved that I could speak with someone else who understood. Although she was dealing with so much of her own pain, she comforted me, and I comforted her. Tears shed together, created such a bond. We no longer felt like strangers.

Throughout our exchange, we could hear the men working on the elevator, all the while assuring us that we'd be ok, and that we'd be out soon. When they finally jimmied the door open, we were still between floors, so they lifted us up about four feet to our floor.

We were so relieved. We thanked them and thanked The Creator for keeping us safe. We promised to visit each other after the kids were home and settled.

I walked to my apartment at the end of the hall, turned the key and pushed. But nothing happened. I looked up at the number to confirm that I was in fact at the right door. I pushed harder, and as the door opened, I could feel a cool breeze coming through and under the door. It felt like a wind tunnel. "But I didn't leave any windows open...",

I thought to myself. As I walked into my apartment, I was amazed at the surreal scene in front of me. It was like something from a movie. My windows, an entire wall of glass, were broken from the wind and storm while we were trapped in the elevator. Everything was soaked and there was glass everywhere, but mostly large shards of glass penetrated the fabric of my favorite chair. What were the chances of something like this happening.

In my mind's eye, I saw myself curled up and sleeping on that chair, after having my shower and my drink, with my book. I can't believe how I prayed for relief, I wanted a way out, I wanted to die. Could someone have been listening to me? Did I almost get what I prayed for, for so long? Dying without guilt. I had thought of so many ways to escape. I thought about my children, I thought that maybe they'd be better off with my mother, my stepmother, their father any one but me. I felt completely useless in their lives. Looking at that scene at that exact moment woke me up. I existed in a heavy fog until that point.

At that moment the storm dissipated, the sun came out and everything became clear. A realization washed over me, there was a God, a higher power, someone was watching over me. It was not my time. I had plenty to live for, my two daughters needed me. I could not possibly leave them. I had been asking for a miracle, and a miracle had just occurred. The hairs on the back of my neck, my head, my arms, stood up. I immediately called my father again on his cell and asked him to turn around again and come upstairs. I ran to my new friend next door. I had to show them this unbelievable scene.

That night I made the decision to pack up and leave that place. It was time for a fresh start. It was time to rebuild. It was ok to start over. I cried and prayed for hours. These tears were different though, they were no longer tears of sorrow. I felt at peace, I felt lighter somehow. I spent the entire night in hugging my children really tight.

Since then I went back to school, became an expert in my field then started and now run a very successful business. I kiss and hug my children everyday. I show them and tell how much I love them everyday. I love and take care of myself everyday. I give thanks everyday. My children and I have made a vow to make a difference in the lives of others everyday. We work hard, love hard and laugh everyday.

BRENDA FOREMAN

LILIA *Esi*

"Walk with the dreamers, the believers, the courageous, the cheerful, the planners, the doers, the successful people with their heads in the clouds and their feet on the ground. Let their spirit ignite a fire within you to leave this world better than when you found it."

- WILFERD PETERSON

Amidst the warmth of the African Sun, facing the ocean, listening to the surfs lulling drum, fishing boats and nets litter the scape, brilliant hues of blues a pretty picture makes. My feet naked of constricting shoes, toes dig into beautiful sandy beach. The structure of the Cape Coast Castle behind me looms, a sign reads "door of no return" hangs in gloom. Through this door millions and millions of enslaved Africans were shoved and loaded onto ships like common goods. Shackled until they reached their destination. Many of them blood relative to me no doubt. That thought overwhelms me to the core. Their DNA runs through my veins. Their survival, a catalyst that resulted in who I've become. It hit me that my purpose was already designed for me, if I were able to have traced my family tree. So standing there on the beach in Ghana, I realized that my purpose started here, to help heal the grief of those whose ancestry started there. Grief can hold on deep and strong and can be carried for generations and generations to come. My purpose is my passion all rolled up in one. One without the other is incomplete.

I have always tried to live with integrity; it's the way that my parents and extended family molded me. I come from a long line of entrepreneurs, who had an enormous social conscience and response. My father owned his own business and apprenticed several young men under his wing, teaching them a trade and business acumen a gift that all still credit him for today. My grandmother, Lister, washed and ironed for a living, through this fostered many children and raised them on her own, with the same love and determination she had for her own children. My grandmother, Lilia, a nurse and midwife, gave birth to babies all over the island she was revered and respected for her dedication and commitment to ensuring that women were safe and had healthy babies despite of the rural, under served communities they lived in. My mother opened one of the first boutiques on the island. She travelled to neighboring islands shopping for products for her store. Her business started a movement for other women to do the same thing. This boosted the economy and employment opportunities for women. Their lives are an example for me; it's their efforts and those of my ancestors that propel me.

In 1978, at age 11, my family and I immigrated to Canada. I was immediately jarred by the changes in culture, climate and social environment. Having been socialized in Dominica, an island whose people are predominantly African descendants, I became immediately aware of issues related to race. For the years following my migration to Canada I struggled and yearned for a deeper connection to community and culture. For the first time I was aware of my color and it sparked the question, why am I here? I heard it daily "Go back to where you came from!" and "Why do you people from the islands leave the hot sun?" there were almost daily attacks on me based on my race; I became ashamed of my hair, my skin, my own face. I became the one all the kids taunted. My soul became lonely, I was haunted by the love of my family and friends I left back home. I was haunted by the memories of a place where I never, ever felt threatened or alone. A powerful community used to support and surround me now, I live in a place where people acted like they hated me.   Even at school, the books I read about Black people were only about enslavement and degradation all throughout the Caribbean and African continent. I felt that this reinforced the reason for the other kids to be so cruel to me. Even then, I always felt that something was missing in the story and I shouldn't use it to define me. Luckily, my father had brought his library from Dominica with him. I re-discovered some of the books I had read at a young age from his collection by Frantz Fannon, Khail Gibran and so on. The weekends were my respite, a few other families moved to Canada around the same time my family did and we all got together almost every weekend. My parents also discovered a Dominican cultural Club who hosted picnics in the summer. Through reintegration with culture and community, I began to find my beauty again.

Around age 16, I came across a group led by Francis Jeffers, a social activist also from Dominica. For a while I was surrounded by the familiar, he formed a club, I found safety and comfort there. I also become more active after high school. A few other Black kids in the community embraced me; I began to feel a little more worthy. At last people with common interests who didn't see skin color or use it as a tool to distress.

I struggled through high school; I think I was culturally depressed, the immigration experience made me feel oppressed. Back then I couldn't name it, but thinking back, I can still feel it. The deep dark feeling of living in a world that's not familiar, the environment, weather, social norms, systems, communication styles, were all so strange and unfamiliar. Toward the end of my high school years in my heart I felt a calling. I felt that my life career was to help others as a social worker.

My guidance counselor tried to dissuade me from this career path. My grades did not coincide with my purpose within the Canadian educational system. My immigration experience made me forget that I was born into a line of entrepreneurs with a strong social conscience. In confusion and not being able to see a future career ahead of me, I went to work right after high school while I thought about my next move.

During that time, even my nuclear family dynamic had shifted. The relationship between my parents had drifted to talk of divorce. The whole family became conflicted. My father eventually left. I never understood divorce or the grief one goes through during and after a divorce until my adult years when I faced one myself.

Two years later, I found myself at Centennial College in a program that failed to inspire the excitement I sought to get that piece of paper I forged on. The summer of 1993, I landed a job at the YMCA Employment Centre. There I found my passion again working with young people who had also been uprooted from their home environment. That summer I thrived. I began to find my beauty again. By the end of my program at Centennial, I was working full time at the YMCA as an employment counselor/Life Skills facilitator.

In 2002, I started working exclusively with Black youth connecting young people with role models, exposing them to career exploration and social activities. The program did more than that, it provided young people an opportunity to shape a positive African Canadian Identity based on historical facts. It exposed them to positive reflections of themselves in the messages they heard, the books they were exposed to and the opportunities that they were encouraged to pursue. As my career unfolded, helping others develop a sense of pride and assisting them to live out their purpose became a theme for me.

This theme was further solidified through my involvement through the African Centered Rites of Passage process expedited by Nene Kwasi Kafele, Joanne Artherly and Sipo Kwaku in 2006. Rites of passage led me to the spiritual connection to Africa that I longed for, a connection that I didn't even recognize. Even though I had already delved deeply into community work, I didn't understand the connection between purpose and my ancestorship. The name is an essential component of the spiritual anatomy of a human being. Thus, from time immemorial, Africans have said in respect to the sacredness of the name: "Truly, without a name the human being does not exist." During slavery and colonization our African names were replaced with foreign names, names that are totally devoid of power or purpose and directly opposed to our spiritual development and endeavours. I now embrace the name Esi. Born on a Sunday. Sunday's child is the passive, sensitive and warm member of the family. She is born for leadership and mediation. Peacemaker.

So as my life journey led me to my purpose, I realized, I have always known, but yet, seemed to have lost connection to it somehow. I believe however, every moment we experience in life is connected to our purpose. Maybe I was born to forget and re-learn why I was created.

There are many, many things left out of my story that could give even more insight into who I am. I fill my days in ways in which I can help heal and build my cultural community. That is where my beauty is found. In living my passion and purpose.

Freedom

I write because it's the only freedom I have as a Black/female/immigrant/ /divorced/childless/manless/racialized/daughter of divorced parents.

Living in a foreign land that 33 years later my soul still cannot assimilate to.

Surviving within isms that bind me systematically. Western cultural penetration serving to sever my cultural anchor from where it is deeply rooted and in where it is deeply rooted.

Feel me?

Through my journey from the slave ship to the boardroom my tongue has been slashed and my psyche has been trashed around

My ethnicity bashed.

Shackled.

Given no air to breathe.

I have become foreign to my own damn self

Culturally.

Even my identity has been flung around becoming hyphenated for so long.

My poems are what free me

Eases me

Builds resilience.

My therapy.

I do not need the further oppression of my words reconstructed in a foreign format

To what my mind creates.

So let

At least

My words be.

Free.

LILIA ESI

LAUREN*Alicia*
Committed To Loving My Design Beyond Damage

"I didn't realize the power of my story until I started telling it to myself."

- LAUREN ALICIA

I've watched broken dreams destroy inspiration, infiltrate perspective, and leave people guessing. Meanwhile, the purpose of our design desperately waited for us to allow our strength to kick in and return, acknowledging its never-ending existence. "The route to success" is not as easy to identify like the graphics that demonstrate climbing the corporate ladder...go figure!

Before I answered *purpose's* call or considered its questions, I made mistakes, went my own way and rebelled EVERY TIME because my route was the best route. I could clearly see in a close distance, instant satisfaction and me living the dreams that I always imagined, so again, my route was the best route.

The thing is, I took the long journey (long to me) to realize it wasn't. I'll start from the beginning... I am the last-born to my then married parents; the first and other child they have together is a boy. I am one of two, making me their second attempt for different decisions; I'll get back to this later.

The first dream that I completely fell in love with is fashion design, and we're still together (although distant). I remember in the third grade being mesmerized by the designs of Tommy Hilfiger, it was popular in 90's Hip Hop. Other kids and myself took our fat markers and used our free time to draw (not sketch) what it would be like to wear Tommy Hilfiger.

I wanted to be a model. It was my life-long dream until the fifth grade...when everything changed. A modeling agency came to town and held a casting. I HAD to be there, this was my shot!! However, my dad forbid it for the sake of my feelings, and my mom pushed back for the sake of my confidence...even though she didn't want me to go either. Anyway, my mother and I went. They did not pick me because I had braces. We went home. I didn't cry, or maybe I did and don't remember the full emotions of that event, it's possible I blocked it out... but worse than that, I was confused. My first real dream in an industry that I can talk about for hours, came to an end because at the time, it was modeling or nothing.

As their second and last child, they trained a passionate person by making me fight for everything I wanted; I don't think they knew that would happen!

The next year in the sixth grade, I re-decided that it wasn't over, and if I could not model the clothes...I WILL DESIGN them, and I completely, full heartily...fell in love with fashion design as an aspiring designer! Not to mention in that same year, the modeling agency called, assuming I didn't have braces anymore... I was over it and them...especially after we found out it was a scam. Live and learn, learn and live. One of the reasons I was able to move on from the dream of modeling and pursue designing was how my sixth grade teacher cultivated through goal-setting, and encouraged our dreams like we were the most talented people she ever met (at least in my head). After looking at one of my wedding dress designs, she told me she wished I were around when she got married because she loved this dress.

I learned from her that sometimes it only takes one time to inspire a dream forever.

Fast-forward to high school where I am still this aspiring fashion designer sketching several designs at least once a month, and dreaming of attending Parsons The New School for Design. The summer before the eleventh grade year began, I signed up to attend their pre-college program for Fashion Design in NYC, it was full. Not to worry, they had another program that made more sense called Design + Management, turns out, it was full too. Still no worries, I said to myself, "next summer I will sign up early and I will get into the Fashion Design pre-college program"...it was full on the first day enrollment opened. However, my second choice, which happened to be purpose's only choice, Design + Management was wide open, just for me!! I was on my way to NYC for the first time at 16 by myself!

The Design + Management program was purpose's choice because it was about business, not design but the design of a business and how to create, maintain and sustain one (something I would need for the future). Students can start any business they want with the knowledge from this program but I just wanted to design. My route was the best route. I loved the summer pre-college program; I really did, it provided amazing information! I still keep in touch with some of the people I met. However, I wanted to design and be perfected by Parsons. So when it came time for college applications, I only applied to Parsons' Fashion Design program like someone came down from Heaven and told me to do that...NOPE! My application for that program was rejected. HA! Purpose - 1:Lauren – 0.

Not to worry, I still don't give up. So I applied to two other schools for Fashion Design, one in NYC and one in LA. Please Note: NYC is my dream city for living. I was finally accepted into the school in LA, and I went. However a family friend knew me to well to let me be in a city that's not NYC, and my last choice. My friend called Parsons, asked why my application wasn't accepted and what I could do to be reconsidered. Well…turns out that my file at Parsons had a note in it, indicating I should have applied to Design + Management because I would have been accepted. I withdrew from the school in LA, got on a plane headed home (I'm from Michigan), I applied to Design + Management (purpose's first and only choice for me), and I was accepted 30 days before classes at Parsons in NYC began.

I graduated four years later with a B.B.A. in 2011. HALLELUJAH!! I finally started listening to purpose…or did I?

There were two job interviews I lined up to stay in NYC after college, and pursue design through a business aspect, it didn't happen. However, because the two jobs were at the same company and one trumped the other in position, and the talent scout never mentioned that my interview was the worst… I knew it was something that I was missing. So I listened to purpose (for the moment), and started writing business proposals as an independent consultant, as exciting as that was it wasn't where I was supposed to be. I am now asking purpose, "WHAT IS GOING ON?" (Yep, I'm frustrated).

I founded GYC-GirlYOUCrazy.com in 2012, a blog + collaborative. It flips the meaning of something playful that can discourage, keeping it playful but using the phrase as fuel to accomplish/complete/finish and live your dream with great expectation and a smile. GYC Girl YOU Crazy exists as an inspiration source, outlet, hand up, support, testimonial release location, fuel station, dream builder, reminder of purpose... whatever you need to move forward and see your dreams, desires of your heart as a reality or help/support to remember or dream a new dream for girls, young women, women at any age!

It became my outlet for staying motivated and away from discouragement in my moment of not knowing. I realized some tell their story after they're this big manifested success but who is willingly to share about the journey while on the journey? It's been amazing!!

But then I got a call from a life insurance agency for a job interview. I was offered a job to be an agent in Michigan and have the financial resources to pursue the real dream...DESIGN!! I struggled with passing the exam for the first time because I really DID NOT want to sell life insurance but I studied too hard to quit. I passed the exam on the second go. Training began, I enjoyed it, I saw how I could help people see life insurance as a necessity and not a luxury but then field training began... and it was depressing.

As much as I want people to be informed about the need for life insurance, that was not going to be the way I went about it, especially since GYC-GirlYOUCrazy.com was uplifting, and I came home crying about people's lives. I quit that job, no thanks. However, it did teach me that when I eventually have employees how to implement life insurance into my benefits so they may have it if/when they move on.

Now back to GYC, blogging opened the door to my honesty and self-discovery, the more I blogged, the more my eyes were open to inspiration. It showed me that the journey of self-discovery is never-ending and purpose will forever teach me this. It allowed me to see the different levels of ME. As much as I love design, I love THE Design that my purpose created for me to handle in each moment. I learned that as much as there is a big dream, there are small and rough dreams on journey to getting there.

With that said, I left out above that at 15, my parents got divorced after 21 years and a few months of marriage. And someone encouraged me to write a book about how to handle it as a child of divorce around the same time. Purpose allowed for ALL of this preparation to bring me here and to keep going even through all the wear and tear I put on my design.

But GYC by the way of purpose reminded me, it birthed in me that "the power of our story could be the key to someone's healing." I stopped all other pursuits because my route IS NOT the best route and I wrote and published, Dear Divorce, Thank You (Even Though I Hate You) Sincerely, My Parents' Grown Kid: A Journey of Hate, Healing and Understanding. It's intended for grown kids of divorce (teen and adult) from ages 15 and up to help process the journey of what it's like to be us.

I stopped running from purpose and I crossed the lines that it asked me to cross. Committed to loving my design beyond damage. Everything that I've done or tried before brought me to this moment I'm in right now, an author, freeing my mind of the past and hesitations without meaning, and leading me into the next.

I am committed to loving my design beyond damage because I am talking about life, mistakes, experiences, the process, the journey and things that may have allowed us to question our worth, the debris of past disappointments that may have provoked or encouraged us to live in fear of what our design is built to fulfill.

Can I be honest with you? I did not want to start this journey off (after college) with everyone knowing my story…most people get famous AND THEN they tell it. I realized that I indulged in bitterness outside of career goals, ignored influence, accused the innocent and took tips from the guilty. But here I am proud to honestly tell my story of how I am my parents' grown kid of divorce and all the junk that comes with that, refusing to ignore and use it to help heal for the sake of sanity and understanding.

The thing you could be running from or are so focused on running to just may be what design was for me, preparation and for the future. Meanwhile, there is a rough dream you may possibly be asked to pursue right now:

> They are the dreams that you know will make you better, and leave an amazing mark on this life but the route that it asks you to take requires you to be more vulnerable than you're comfortable with… but they are the dreams that put the notches in your belt and confidence in your stride for what's next!

I opened myself up to see all the possibilities and levels of me, and my inner compass began to speak as THE voice of reason and the microphone of my truth:

Your success already exists; it waits in the purpose that you persist. Believe and continue to pursue. The question is… Will you think beyond a thought? Go outside of what is inside… taking what is inside, OUT!

Commit and Love the purpose of your design beyond any damage you take it through because there is no amount of mistakes, or thoughts that WE CAN have about thinking we know the best route that will hinder purpose from pursuing us.

JANÉT *Aizenstros*
Media: A Tribute To Finding Passion and Purpose

"My mission in life is not merely to survive, but to thrive; and to do so with some passion, some compassion, some humor, and some style."

- MAYA ANGELOU

The Raise of the Guardians happens to be one of my favorite child movies ever. The story of Jack Frost teaches a powerful lesson about knowing your CENTER. Throughout the movie, Santa Claus, questions Jack Frost by asking, " Jack Frost, what is your center?!"

I believe this movie is so relatable to entrepreneurs who embark on their life-path of passion and purpose. Many who decide to travel on this journey at times compare themselves to someone else who they perceive is further along in the journey.

Many of you reading have probably thought the following comments:
"How come they are more successful than I am?"
"How come they are able to accomplish more than I can?"
"How come I can't move as quickly as they are?"

This monkey-chatter in our heads is what many of us self-sabotage our minds with repeatedly. Yet, the question I would ask is, "why do we have to compare ourselves to anyone else?"

I remember when women who had no concept of the services my business offered would seek me out to share with me that we had similar businesses. Yet, once I started researching their company I would discover, yes we both inspire, yet, we are still very different. Or they thought I was a motivational speaker or they thought I was whatever label they could place on me to define what they believed was my purpose. This caused me to become extremely intentional in defining who I was as a person and what I wanted convey in my business. What message I discovered in becoming intentional is that it made me realize, I do not care what labels people wanted to place on me or expected for me to be. I was going to be ME!

I believe the moment you start comparing yourself to another person means you've lost focus on what is your CENTER.

What I have discovered is when you are firmly rooted in knowing your center you don't need to question, compare or feel insecure in where you are on your life-path. Or what speed you are going at to get you to your allotted destination?!

I will admit in the beginning after studying to become a life coach, I travelled down the road of many life coaches by starting an online coaching business. I did this because many of the gurus (who are my friends) recommended I do exactly what they had done. They explained how lucrative it was to have an online coaching program. Yet, in this pursuit of becoming an online guru, I soon discovered I wasn't really enjoying the process of conveying my message in this manner. The result left me feeling like my business was a chore instead of empowering those who sought my services. I was unhappy because I knew at my core it wasn't what I really wanted to do.

One day while observing my children, I began thinking about all the things I loved doing in my childhood. I began thinking about what activities currently in my life that gave me pleasure. I began listening to my own conversations with myself and with people to gage what inspired me. Soon, I realized that I loved books, writing, and music. Truly, I love most things artistic. I recalled a book I wrote when I was seventeen called My Heart, Open as the Sky. For some undefined reason in my life, I always went back to this book when I felt depressed or needed to feel inspired. I believe this book has been an emotional refuge for me throughout my journey. This book has been a tool of healing, a feeling of accomplishment and perceived disappointment of dreams deferred.

Meanwhile, my coaching practice was geared towards business due to my extensive business background, I spent very little time talking to the women who called me about business.   Primarily, the conversations I had with many of the women who contacted would veer off into conversations on spirituality, human existence, religion, all aspects of relationships. What I really loved speaking to them about was how they could build an amazing business while having great relationships and maintaining an amazing lifestyle.   Meanwhile, the topic of relationships at that point in my life felt difficult for me to offer advice due to the fact I was going through my own life transition with my marriage.   Finally, in a one on one coaching session with my coach, I shared my apprehension about offering advice on relationships. As swiftly as I made that statement, she got a hold of me and said, "Janet, stop it! Why would you ever say that! When I listen to you and your life experiences I think of you as, 'Everything Girl'!" As I sat on the other side of the phone perplexed by this statement, I responded back "Everything Girl! What do mean by that statement, everything girl!"

She explained, that my life has given me the opportunity to be in all sorts of relationships. I've been the Carrie Bradshaw single girl. The girl who lives together with a man she's not married too. The girl who has a child out of wedlock and then marries the man who she was living with out of wedlock and whom is the father or her child. Then another relationship transition would be us separating, then divorcing and now I am single again yet this time with children. Surprisingly, she was right. I had never really looked at my relationship history that way. She further explained why women find me so relatable. She stated, "Janét, you are not merely just offering an opinion to these women you're conversing with, you've lived those experiences.

Our conversation that day awakened me to something deeper about myself. It brought me back to a place of remembering the power of sharing your story. I soon discovered that, meanwhile, I have a tremendous amount of business experience, I wasn't passionate about talking about the details of putting a business together. I was passionate about talking about the life elements which is everything around the business that holds a business together. My defining moment in my business happened when I realized what message I wanted to speak and teach women. It was about relationships. I believe relationships is one of the foundational elements that holds businesses together. I love talking about the relationships we have with ourselves, other people and how our purpose affects the overall societal collective.

Yet, my coach's purpose for making that statement "Janet, you are Everything Girl!" It was not to spark me to go out the next day and start a coaching business focused on relationships. Oh no! It was to ignite the passion within me to guide me back to my CENTER.

Also, I believe it opened me up to ask other questions that many of us are afraid to ask which is "WHO ARE YOU and what do you believe?"

Finally, I realized why women speak to me about their most intimate details it's not just that they trust and value my opinion. I believe their trust comes from my ability to share my most vulnerable moments with them. While allowing myself to be possibly judged by them and everyone else listening or reading my content. I am a student of the teachings by the Taoist Lao Tzu, living by his quote,, "I show my weakness, to show my strength."

This new found awareness propelled me to look at my company with an entirely different perspective. What I discovered is I knew I loved inspiring women, yet, I didn't want to partake in the traditional coaching platform as many of my peers. Meanwhile, there is nothing wrong with wanting to be traditional, I decided to take my life coaching knowledge and use it in a different manner. I knew the format I was seeking would have to be ever-changing, remove any opportunity for boredom and moved like me -- at lightning speed.

I began reflecting on all the elements I derived inspiration from as a child to present. I loved books, I loved designing elements to look certain way, I loved talking, sharing, inspiring and being inspired by other people. Now, all I needed was to figure out how to find a platform I could house all of my inspiration under that would allow me to do everything I loved in a cohesive manner.

What I found was MEDIA!

It was ever-changing, moved quickly and the opportunity to create multiple formats in different platform styles was an endless way to turn my dreams into a reality.

Media is the element I channeled my inspiration and when combined with my passion for women has become my life purpose obsession. I live it. Breathe it. Can't live without it. This is my CENTER. Through this platform I have been able to incorporate all things I love such as publishing books, interactive media design and broadcasting. These elements have allowed me to do what I do best which is explore myself, aid people in exploring their lives and helping them to create what they want to experience for their lives.

The RESULT?!

Now, I have passionate conversations daily with people all over the world talking about business, love and lifestyle.

I will affirm that when you know your purpose, you will work the endless hours, toss everything to the wayside at times because your passion can be all-consuming. I am not saying you don't have to maintain balance. I've redefined how to create wholeness on my journey. Yet, what I have truly discovered is that my CENTER has become a surreal elixir that is necessary on those days when perceived obstacles come to test my stance. Or the days I feel like I want to give up like the character, Ordinary from Bruce Wilkinson's book the Dream Giver, as he battled his obstacles in the "LAND OF THE GIANTS."

Yet, through it all, the most profound realization is truly understanding that I am the guardian over my sacred CENTER. It assures me daily the vital importance of knowing who am I by firmly grounding myself with those who possess a heart most common.

My question to all of you reading is, what is your CENTER?

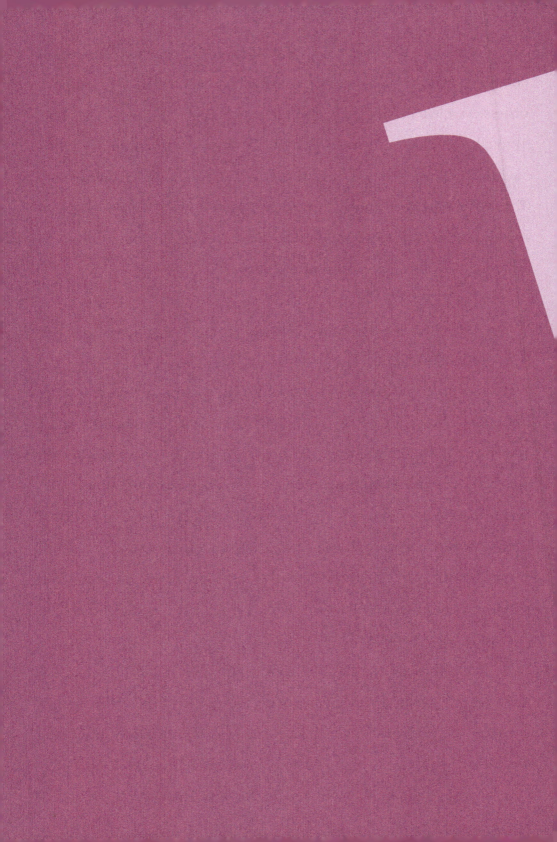

YASHEEKA SUTTON

COMPANY: *The E.L.L.E Foundation Inc.*

WEBSITE: *About.me/YaSheekaSutton*

EMAIL: *TheElleFoundation@gmail.com*

RAMONA OSTRANDER

COMPANY: *REALTOR®, RE/MAX Real Estate Centre Inc., Brokerage*

WEBSITE: *CallRamona.com*

EMAIL: *Ramona4RealEstate@gmail.com*

TAMARA GARRISON-THOMAS

COMPANY: *Garrison Prosperity Solutions Enterprises*

WEBSITE: TamaraGarrisonThomas.com

EMAIL: *Tamara@garrisonprosperitysolutions.com*

TRUDY DIXON

COMPANY: *Personal Trainer/ Triathlon Coach*

WEBSITE: *MakeTimePT.wix.com/maketimept*

EMAIL: *TrudyDixon@yahoo.com*

SHARON SMITH STEWART

COMPANY: *SharonAnn Marie*

WEBSITE: *SharonAnnMarie.com*

EMAIL: *info@sharonannmarie.com*

MOIRA SUTTON

COMPANY: *Determine, Discover and Transform Your Life™*

WEBSITE: *SuccessBreakthrough.com*

EMAIL: *MSutton@successbreakthrough.com*

KEITIAUNNA HOWARD

COMPANY: *Successful Single Moms, LLC*

WEBSITE: *SingleMomsSuccessTour.com*

EMAIL: *SuccessfulSingleMoms@gmail.com*

BRENDA FOREMAN

COMPANY: *BStyled by Brenda Foreman*

WEBSITE: *BStyled.ca*

EMAIL: *info@bstyled.ca*

CAROLYN DICKINSON

COMPANY: *SuperMom Entrepreneur*

WEBSITE: *SuperMomEntrepreneur.com*

EMAIL: *SuperMomEntrepreneur@gmail.com*

INDEX

LAUREN ALICIA

COMPANY: *Author of Dear Divorce, Thank You (Even Though I Hate You) Sincerely, My Parents' Grown Kid: A Journey of Hate, Healing and Understanding*

WEBSITE: *DearDivorceThankYou.com*

EMAIL: *DearDivorceThankYou.Book@gmail.com*

JANÉT AIZENSTROS

COMPANY: *Janét Aizenstros Omni Media Inc.*

WEBSITE: *Janet-Aizenstros.com*

EMAIL: *Info@Janet-Aizenstros.com*

LOVE+*lifestyle*
M E D I A   G R O U P

AVANT GARDE INTELLECTUAL INSPIRATION
...where luxury and intellectualism find cohesion.

  SHIRA Tinok & Tinoket OLAM AHAVA

www.lovelifestylemedia.com

LOVE + Lifestyle Media Group is a virtual publishing house that makes the book creation process effortless for authors that want to create a lasting impression.

Our self-publishing custom design firm offers books in paperback, hardcover and digital formats with worldwide distribution.

Editorial | Design | Print | Marketing | PR | Distribution

info@lovelifestylemedia.com

©2011-2014 LOVE + Lifestyle Media Group.
Janét Aizenstros Omni Media Inc. All Rights Reserved.

Our dedication to quality writing, innovative storytelling is to shift the voice of women in our society.

Our dedication to quality writing, innovative storytelling in our books is to propel women forward in our society. At Ahava Chai, our commitment to quality content allows us to be selective in our book selection process. We publish books that are reflective of our brand and align with our mission. Women deserve to read books that inspire, resonate and compel them to create their own uniqueness.

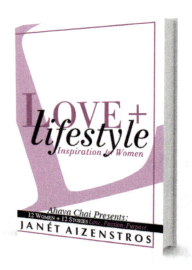

LOVE + LIFESTYLE INSPIRATION FOR WOMEN, the upcoming 2015 compilation series is looking to feature women who are aspiring to live a life full of love, passion and purpose while building phenomenal brands.

They discuss overcoming obstacles, fear, pressing through circumstances, finding security in one's self while becoming empowered women today. They are sharing these stories to help women realize they can overcome any perceived challenge in life and truly create what they want to experience.

To be a part of this compilation, please contact: info@lovelifestylemedia.com.

LOVE+LIFESTYLE
INSPIRATION FOR WOMEN

CPSIA information can be obtained at www.ICGtesting.com
Printed in the USA
LVOW05s0246020515

436943LV00017B/91/P